Lady Candi,

Continue to be Fabulous!!

7

Simple Ways to Shape Your Marriage

Strategies to Feeling Loved & Connected

SHARON J. LAWRENCE, LCSW-C

Thanks, Sharon

ISBN: 9781726712781

Cover Design & Editing by Womack Consulting Group, LLC
Book Cover Photo Credit (Front): Peggie Brokenbrough, Latrell & Will Johnson
Book Cover Photo Credit (Back): ACGP Photography, Russell Young

Dedication

This book is dedicated to my Husband, Rossonio, Our Children, Godchildren, Granddaughter, Godparents, and Family.

Honey, thank you for your encouragement and your faith in my ability when I was scared to step out. You challenged me to have faith and trust God. I am glad you did. I love being your wife and having you with me every step of the way.

Thank you to my Godparents who showed me what true love looks like and for giving me access to see you in your element while working through many challenges. I watched your faith and your works. This alone has influenced me to no end.

To Our Children, Godchildren, and Granddaughter who witness my love for my husband and see me happy daily; it is my goal to always reflect a healthy relationship so that you can believe and honor the purpose of marriage. I hope to make you proud always.

Introduction

If you are reading this book, you are curious about ways to improve your marriage (or relationship). Whether you are seriously dating, engaged or married, the principles in this book can apply. So, do not drop the book wondering if it will add value to your life and relationship. I promise you that it will, if you are open to receiving this valuable information.

If you are anything like me, you will find that you are often seeking ways to improve or strengthen your relationship with your mate. For some of us, we were preparing years before we met our mates or spouses.

I can recall for many years, how I would call my Godmother to tell her about my moments of feeling as if I had lost my wedding ring. Let's be clear, I was not married during this time and did not wear a ring on my ring finger. My Godmother would remind me that this sensation was because I was going to be married one day. I believed her and my faith was what carried me to stand firm on her message and God's promises to me.

My twenties and early to mid-thirties were uncomfortable at times because of the wait for that special someone. When asked if I was married, my response would always be, "not yet!" If someone came back with a response like, "how do you know if you will ever get married?" My response was always, "I know I will. I am someone's wife and someone's mother." This would stun people but that did not stop me from believing and preparing to be a wife one day.

Trust me, there were moments in my single years when I became weary in my waiting. At times, I experienced sadness as a result of others' response to me still being single as if I was a lost cause or as if something was wrong with me. In my private time with God, I would ask if my memo and request had been received while tears ran down my face. Once I concluded my prayer, I was sure to let God know how much I trusted Him with my life and my journey despite my feelings.

Even though it was my desire to be married, I was also determined to enjoy my single life. I witnessed married people who would constantly complain about marriage and would actually tell single people not to get married. When this happened, it was my mission to avoid all forms of negative messaging such as this while waiting.

I surrounded myself with couples who represented the type of marriage I wanted to have one day. I watched how they treated one another and I appreciated their transparency in my presence. From them, I gleaned the tools and principles needed for a healthy relationship.

As a single person, I also read The Power of a Praying® Woman by Stormie Omartian, which was and continues to be a dynamic book. So dynamic, that as a single person, I also purchased and read multiple times, The Power of a Praying® Wife. Every time I picked up this book, it was not just about reading, it was about the daily prayer devotional that allowed me to pray for multiple areas that would impact my future spouse. I used this daily prayer devotional in preparation for MY husband and for myself.

This book is great for any couple, regardless of your relationship stage. I am confident that faith and effective tools will prepare you for a successful relationship.

Let's fast forward a little. In 2013, I met my husband on an online dating site called Plenty of Fish©. Yes, you got it right. We met online.

Believe it or not, my beloved Auntie Rosetta, who was 72 years old at the time, suggested that I try online dating. I finally signed up for Plenty of Fish© after hearing about it from a former colleague. I may have been on the site, all of three to six weeks before I met my husband. Over the course of those weeks, I had two dates prior to meeting my husband... well, actually one and a half. The half date was with a minister from Baltimore who invited me on a date, but the day before, he insisted that it was not a date. He then proceeded to imply that I was catfishing him (blank stare). He insisted that I weighed more than my recent pictures portrayed. I didn't.

He would spend the entire phone call either talking about himself or giving me a compliment that would only match if we were actually in a relationship. By the time the *non-date* day came about, I showed up for only 5 minutes, introduced myself and let him know that I had made other plans since it was not a date. I dressed super cute and it was my birthday!! I did not tell him that. I kept it moving. By the time I heard from him again, I was married.

The second guy never asked me anything about my personal or professional life and kept giving me compliments. We went to the movies once and while saying goodbye at my car, I noticed a big bug on my trunk. He was afraid of the bug. In that moment, I knew it was not going to work. I needed someone who could handle a bug. I gave him a friendly and quick hug and bid him farewell.

Now, Mr. Lawrence was my third and final date from Plenty of Fish©. In preparation for our first date, I would only text him. He wanted to call, but for two weeks leading up to the date, I refused to talk on the phone because of my experience with the first two guys. I figured that if he was going to do something strange or inappropriate via text then I would not have to actually talk to him. Funny, huh? Let's just say that he never said anything inappropriate… or weird… during our text communication. I was hopeful. I decided that I would create an application with a series of questions to give him when we met.

On our first date, which went extremely well, I presented him with the application in a sealed envelope at the end of the date and requested that he only open it, answer the questions and return it to me if he was interested in being in a relationship with me. To make a very long story short, my husband completed the application and we were an official couple within two weeks of our first date. Nine months later we were married. My husband proposed and we were engaged for only two hours. I should let you know that he planned our entire wedding because I did not want a wedding. We have been intentionally happily married since June 14, 2014.

If you wish to view the 2-hour proposal and wedding, please feel free to visit the following link:
https://youtu.be/oC8YsBPDmEY

Now, that you know a little about me, I want you to know that by writing this book, it allows me to share some simple ways to help shape your marriage based on being intentional. I hope you enjoy.

Quick Lesson About Being Intentional

Since meeting my husband in 2013, I have to admit that I have learned a great deal about myself, marriage, and the importance of intentionality.

According to the Merriam-Webster Dictionary, the word 'intentional' means done on purpose; deliberate.

In my marriage, my husband and I, along with our faith, work diligently to be intentional about our actions towards each other. It is not always perfect but we know of its importance in a relationship.

As a Licensed Clinical Social Worker and Therapist for Therapists, Professionals and Couples, I also stress the importance of being intentional in my work with couples. If I can get them to see the purpose of intentionality along with the benefits it can bring, then my job is done and they are on a great journey towards a happy marriage.

Do not get me wrong, I am not saying that we are always intentional. What I am saying is that being intentional goes a long way when you are seeking to strengthen any relationship. And, when it is not a perfect moment, you have enough good times to remind you of your ability to work towards healing in your relationship.

Recently, a client asked me to give a clear definition of intentional in comparison to being structured and organized. They wanted to know what was the difference. This is my explanation. When you are structured and organized, you are mostly on automatic. It is what you do a lot of times without prompting. It is about routine. There is a feeling that sets in when your metabolism kicks in and your focus becomes more about productivity.

When intentionality is present, it has everything to do with your desire to act or do despite your feelings in the moment. It is about having a purposeful response to your mate. Your vows and commitment to one another should drive your intention. Your heart and level of respect for one another should also drive your intention.

The word intention is not used enough in this context. It is often referenced when talking about intent vs. actions in situations where a person feels that they have been offended or wronged. This is a good area to discuss further, but it is not the same intention that I am referring to for the purpose of this book.

Intentionality will be referenced a great deal in this book and it is my hope that you will gain a greater understanding.

This book is not rocket science. It is a simple reminder or a quick teaching tool for those who need some help in the areas of building a better marriage.

By this time, I am sure you are ready to receive some of the amazing ways to shape your marriage. Being hungry and thirsty for tools is what's needed to strengthen your relationship. Daily, even on my most tired days, I give my all even if my husband tries to give me a pass. I appreciate him for his love, patience and how he always strives to give all of himself to me.

Now, that my heart is fluttering as I talk about Mr. Lawrence, I realize it is time to get into sharing the 7 Simple Ways to Shape Your Marriage. Let's get it!!

Contents

Way #1:

Love Unconditionally

Love Unconditionally

Proverbs 3:3-4 (NIV): "Let love and faithfulness never leave you; bind them around your neck, write them on the tablet of your heart. Then you will win favor and a good name in the sight of God and man."

To function unconditionally means that there are no conditions attached. To say that you love unconditionally means, that you love through the good, the bad, and the ugly.

Loving unconditionally is to love without stipulations changing. Often, in relationships, if a person does something to offend or disappoint the other member of the partnership, it is followed with doubt about their love for that person. This is something that we have to be careful of. In relationships, there is a commitment that should be regarded often. When this does not happen, you find yourself questioning the other person's love for you in moments of disappointment.

To elaborate on this further, let's liken it to a wife forgetting an important date related to her husband thereby causing him to question her love for him. The reality may be that she truly forgot and that it has nothing to do with their love or how she feels about him. However, the husband is left to his own thoughts and feelings. He thinks he is no longer respected, regarded or valued. He carries these thoughts and feelings until they are able to discuss this matter fully to a place of resolve.

Unfortunately, until there is resolution of past concerns, during moments of reflection you may use this opportunity to bring up unresolved situations that will be coupled with the initial concern. When you decide to bring all of these concerns to the table at once, this is called "layering." This means that you are expressing more than one concern at a time and the original concern is now at the bottom of the pile where it should not be. It should be the main focus of your discussion.

I encourage my couples to focus on a single issue and not to introduce new or past concerns that can strengthen the one presenting issue. This is called being "single focused."

Single Focused is the ability to deal with one concern at a time and not layer. When you consciously or unconsciously layer, you will find that the original concern gets buried under the newly presented issue(s).

Remaining focused means that you are now able to focus on the current issue with love and understanding as well as the goal of resolution. When this skill is mastered, you also maneuver within the entire relationship with love!! When communicating, the ability to unconditionally love also provides a level of safety within a relationship. The ability to find the good, to acknowledge areas that need improvement, to perceive and receive information with no judgment and to see your partnership as the most important relationship you will ever have will have a great impact on your future together.

When I think of my husband, I think of our vows and our friendship. Although, I am trained as a clinician to see individuals and couples, I am not exempt from using the tools and strategies needed to strengthen my own marriage. The ways that are being presented in this book are simple and straight to the point. However, the hard work comes from your intentionality within your relationship.

Please note, that I am not perfect nor have I perfected this, but I am intentional and believe with every fiber of my being that we are committed to loving each other unconditionally.

Relationships come with risks and at times uncertainty, but one thing that you should never be uncertain about is your love for one another. Let this area of love unconditional, be one that is stable and a staple for years to come. It will not be easy but know that when it becomes difficult, you have the desire to work through it with no hesitation.

If this information is new or foreign to you, not only will you have to be intentional about it, but it is necessary to be connected and consistent. There may be moments of pain, but working intentionally allows for these moments of discomfort to be the exception and not the norm. The norm reflected over time will become your unconditional love for one another.

Always remember, loving unconditionally is finding the strength always to allow your hearts to remain connected.

Exercise #1:

- Before moving on to the next section, spend 15-30 minutes with your spouse discussing what unconditional love and what being intentional means to your marriage.
- Determine what needs you and your spouse may have and then discuss how you can meet those needs as it relates to unconditional love.

Notes:

_____

_____

_____

_____

_____

_____

_____

_____

Way #2:

Let Patience
Guide You

Let Patience Guide You

Ephesians 4:2 (NIV): "Be completely humble and gentle; be patient, bearing with one another in love."

If you are not a patient person, this is just for you. It will motivate and encourage you in your time spent with your mate.

I chose to write about patience because when it comes to this area, I had to work my hardest. Yes, me… the clinician and super cool wife. Did I mention, that I am also sweet, kind, funny and helpful? Well, that is me and then there are some other characteristics to puff up my image. This statement alone should make you laugh.

Throughout my life, I worked hard to get things done. Many times, those things did not come when I wanted them to. They came when God wanted to provide. I learned early on, not to pray for patience. The more I prayed for patience in a particular area, the more I felt tortured in waiting for it to happen. It was a terrible feeling.

What was interesting is that I had no problem helping others wait on something or encouraging them. I also had no problem, waiting on others (let's be clear, I am not referring to family and those closest to me. LOL) to get things done. Let me explain.

I found early on in my marriage that I had the ability to be patient with everyone outside of my home and family, but when it came to getting things done that involved me waiting on my husband and family, I was very impatient. This was one of those areas of my life, that I realized that the more I prayed for it, the harder it was to achieve and experience. Having patience was extremely difficult for me.

I had to get things done in a timely manner. It was all about productivity and accomplishing tasks. This not only meant that I found it very difficult to wait but it also reflected that I did not trust them, even though my language said

I did. I was failing horribly in this area. It was so bad that I made people feel uncomfortable. Trust me, knowledge is power. In understanding this character flaw, I was able to increase my self-awareness and introduce intentionality into my personal life and my thinking!

I have not been 100% reformed. However, I am 100% aware. In being aware, I am able to check myself for the betterment of my relationships with those I love.

Now, that I have shared a little about myself, understand that being patient means allowing people to function at their own pace whether it is storytelling, completing chores, tending to personal matters, or movement within other areas.

Patience also means respecting your mates' movement and personality. Yes, I used the word *respect*. You cannot have patience without respect.

I can recall times when I would complete tasks simply because my husband was not moving fast enough for me. I thought I was getting the work done faster, but the message he received was that I was not patient and I did not respect him. It also gave the impression that I did not need him. The reality is that I needed him more than he and I both realized.

In relationships, people fail to realize that their actions are also a part of how their love is shown. Your patience indicates *kindness* and *interest* in your mate.

There you have two more words to join Patience... Kindness and Interest. These words provide the boost for the action of patience to be manifested with intentionality.

Please understand that your intentions cannot be contingent upon your mate's actions. I know this is challenging. Many of you are already saying, "I am only acting this way or do this if they act a certain way." Thinking this way will only create additional conflict and misunderstanding.

It is imperative that you learn that you are with that person for what you can give to that relationship, not what that person can do for you. For example, remember when I talked about knowing that I was someone's wife in my single years? Well, I knew I had a lot to offer and that I would be a good and loving wife. If you know the why and what behind your relationship, there will be an overflow from their love and actions in return. You will get all you need in your relationship when your intentions and actions are gifted daily through patience, respect, kindness, and interest.

Remember that patience is good and that it is necessary. It is required to shape your marriage toward a place of wholeness. Do not pray for patience with no action involved. It must be intentional and it is necessary. Work through the pain of impatience, to ensure that you are practicing patience, respect, love, kindness, and interest. Let patience be a guide in your relationship.

Exercise:

- The next time you ask your spouse to complete a task, stand by and allow them to follow through without any interference or judgment. Refrain from taking on the task yourself. Remain patient and encouraging.

Notes:

_____

_____

_____

_____

_____

_____

_____

_____

_____

_____

Way #3:

No Days Off

No Days Off

> ***Romans 12:10 (NIV):*** *"Be devoted to one another in love. Honor one another above yourselves."*

There is a reason why I tell single people to enjoy their single life. When you get married, there are no days off! That exclamation point is not for yelling, but solely for making a point. You are married every day!! And every day, you are Honoring, Understanding and Respecting your commitment to one another.

Recently, I had the opportunity to speak at a local church on Spiritual Companionship. I highlighted the importance of intentionality. A word which you have seen multiple times already in this book and will see again throughout your reading.

Spiritual Companionship according to the Building Blocks to A Strong Marriage, ©RBC Ministries, is about, "making a spiritual journey through life together, walking hand in hand as children of God toward the wonderful eternity with God that awaits them." Of all of the areas that I spoke on related to mental health, finances, emotional well-being, parenting, sexual intimacy, family history, relationship roles and expectations, the one that covered and molded the discussion for all of these topics was the area related to Spiritual Companionship.

Spiritual Companionship is about being on a journey together and having a oneness that causes you to think alike. In order for you to fully commit to this, you have to be ready and committed. Everyday.

Any person wanting to be single while married or feeling like you need a break from the marriage puts the marriage and relationship in jeopardy of not only ending prematurely but can lead to one dishonoring the commitment made to God and one another. You run the risk of introducing toxic barriers to having a healthy and whole relationship.

It is disheartening to hear someone mention the need to get away. Let me make a clarifying statement... unless there is domestic violence, infidelity or behaviors that place you at risk of being harmed, you are obligated to your marriage.

A person who is committed and actually enjoys their marriage, most likely enjoyed their single years. If you are single and reading this book, I ask that you take your time and enjoy your single years before getting married. I do not want you to have any regrets or resentment towards your future spouse. The last thing you want is to spend your married days wishing you were single and resenting your mate as if they are at fault for your lack of happiness. You are the only person responsible for your happiness. Your spouse should be adding to the happiness that is already established.

Now, that I have shared this information, think of your vows and your commitment as a spouse. It is a position that you hold and honor. It is a status that is taken seriously. It is the job that you want for a lifetime. Which means that there are no breaks and no days off.

You are probably wondering if I am referring to trips alone and activities with friends and other family members. No. I am not referring to places, people or things. I am referring to a mindset and the language that accompanies that mindset. You can take as many solo trips and excursions with the ladies or the guys as long as there is an agreement and understanding with your spouse. Just remember that you are part of a team. Team Marriage.

Team marriage is part of this hashtag movement along with other hashtags such as #wife #husband #happylife #marriageworks and so on. These hashtags are used freely, but it is imperative that your language and behavior is strengths-based and filled with intentional, intensified and true love, especially when no one is watching.

The commitment to your marriage is like wearing your status. Please wear this status proudly. Keep is sacred. Honor it always. Do not take any days off. Remember, it is about your mindset and the language you use that strengthens that mindset.

Exercise:

- Create a Date Night Jar where you both contribute ideas of things you can do as a couple. By conducting a simple internet search, you can find steps to create a date night jar. Make sure that your ideas are different from what you would normally do as a couple.

Notes:

_____

_____

_____

_____

_____

_____

_____

_____

_____

Way #4:

Let Laughter
Be a Staple

Let Laughter Be a Staple

> *Psalm 126:2 NIV:* *"Our mouths were filled with laughter, our tongues with songs of joy. Then it was said among the nations, "The Lord has done great things for them."*

All of my younger life, my sisters would tell me that I was "corny." If you are not familiar with this term, it means that your jokes are not funny. That simple. When my sisters would say that, I would still laugh because I felt my jokes were hilarious.

As I have gotten older, some people still say that I am corny but they laugh. Maybe not at my jokes, but they are laughing at and with me. This is the same in my marriage. I am way more serious than my husband, who loves laughing, joking, and surprising people. Even though I am more serious and reserved than him, I enjoy the level of laughter we both bring to our marriage even if I'm not as funny.

My husband has been in the military for 32 years and counting. He has been deployed three times and was in the midst of the Virgin Islands Category 5 Hurricane in 2017. Through all that he has witnessed in his career, I am in awe of how he manages to laugh and enjoy life. He is bothered when people take things too seriously.

There are so many things that could interrupt his sleep and mental health, but he has such a jovial attitude and countenance that his life is constantly filled with joy. When people see him, they see a party. This is every day, at home, at work, and in the neighborhood. He is of the mindset that nothing should be so serious that you are unable to laugh a little.

I love this about our relationship. It is filled with laughter. To laugh is a sign of joy and satisfaction. Learn to find satisfaction in each other and your relationship. Laughter alone has the ability to ward off negative thoughts and foolishness.

My husband and I describe our relationship as fun. I must add that we are a great team. As a result of me being the more serious team member, it creates balance. There is an understanding of who handles what and when. However, when we are unsure, it requires planning to get back on track with fun included.

Allowing laughter to become a staple in your life is welcoming a balance of functioning. Laughter often comes from communicating. If you are communicating about the great, the good, and the challenging, you are doing well.

If you are only communicating when there is conflict you are missing out on having good times with one another. This means that you are lacking what would be a lifestyle of healthy communication. Unfortunately, there are many couples who only talk when there is a concern, other than that they are not expressing themselves as often as they should. Communication should be something that is constantly present.

I encourage my couples to talk often when together. When there is constant communication, it creates a bond and closeness in your marriage. It also allows you to see your mates silly and vulnerable side.

This is something that has to be developed if it does not exist in your relationship. If it is something that you experienced early on in your relationship but it no longer exists, I want to challenge you to work on creating this balance again.

The only way it can be done is to be intentional in your actions and communication. It must be a shared vision and mission to enhance this area of your relationship.

Be creative by introducing silliness to your marriage. For example, my husband and I had a water gun fight in our first apartment. I remember going to the store early that morning to purchase giant water guns. Afterward, I went to work and planned to get off early so that I could beat him home. I filled the water guns and placed his water gun along with the note on a chair by the door. It was the first thing he noticed when he arrived. When he entered the apartment, I knew he had arrived because of the security system saying, "don't forget to take out the trash." That is what we set it to so that he would never forget to take out the trash. I still laugh about that. However, back to the water gun story. I positioned myself and the water fight commenced. I lost what would probably be the best and shortest water fight ever. Oh, you want to know how? I actually lost from laughing too hard and therefore was not fast enough. This is the first time that I have admitted to losing. I will never admit that to him. Maybe when he reads this book, he will miss this page.

Try being creative to keep laughter in your marriage as much as possible. My husband says, "no one wants to be with a person who is either too serious or mad all of the time." I completely agree. You cannot be serious all of the time.

Learn to laugh with your partner. Learn to laugh at yourself and not take things so seriously. Let laughter be often.

Learning to make laughter a staple in your marriage/relationship is necessary but it cannot be forced. Do not try to force your partner to perform on demand. Allow it to be natural. Keep in mind, you do not have to be a comedian (even though, my husband thinks he is). Allow yourself to enjoy the little things and allow laughter to be a part of your relationship.

Whether you are introducing or reacclimating laughter into your relationship, always remember it is necessary and just good to have. Experiencing joy through laughter can be accomplished by doing some of the following:

- Identify one activity a month (in-home or community) to participate in as a team.
- Once a day, when telling about your day, attempt to give information that

has some humor. The goal is to talk about the good, the humorous and the challenging experiences of your day. Let your spouse see you laugh and joke.

- Visit a theme park, comedy show or even go roller skating. Falling down on skates will definitely cause you both to laugh (and may hurt a little).
- Schedule a series of dance lessons. I hope you have some good moves.
- Create a Game Night once a month. Ladies, make sure you pick the games!!! Men cheat. Just a tip!! (Just kidding, Guys!)

These are just a small number of ideas to get you started. I hope you are laughing at these ideas as you picture yourself and your spouse's responses to these ideas. Do not feel obligated to do any of these, but be very intentional about generating a list of ideas to bring about a newness in your relationship in addition to laughter.

Oh, one more thing…please plan these activities with your spouse. This list can and should only come from the two of you working together. Your goal is to partner in creating a list that encourages the presence of laughter in your relationship. Now, go forth and laugh!

Exercise:

- Plan a game night or one of the ideas listed above within the next 30 days.

Notes:

Way #5:

Increase Communication with Eye Contact

Increase Communication with Eye Contact

__Psalm 19:14 (NIV):__ *"May these words of my mouth and this meditation of my heart be pleasing in your sight, Lord, my Rock and my Redeemer."*

Picture This!... Everywhere... 2018... couples are not aware that they are not looking at each when they are having a conversation. (If you are not a Golden Girls Series fan, then the opening of this chapter completely went over your head. No worries, keep reading. Only true fans will get it).

When communicating, couples are either on their cell phones, tending to other tasks and/or focusing on something else in the room.

Communicating with eye contact can be very challenging when you have been communicating a certain way for so long. I can remember learning how to do this. What I found was a sense of safety when communicating with my husband. Now

Ladies, if it is football season, it may not work. I would like to say that I am just kidding, but keep in mind, when football and basketball are on you may not get their undivided attention. When communicating about things especially if it is important, timing is everything.

It is key that you and your spouse know one another to the point, that you can gauge when it is best to communicate about a concern.

This is important. However, many will disagree and say it should not matter what time of day or night, you should be able to have a discussion. What I am saying is, do not place unrealistic expectations on yourself and your spouse when it comes to timing and communicating critical matters. What I will emphasize is that you should not allow it to become one of those unresolved lingering issues that creates added stress.

Now, that I have gotten that part out of the way, let's talk about the necessary face-to-face communication.

In my work with couples, I encourage them to look into each other's eyes when communicating in sessions and when they are alone. Most couples (not all) respond with, "this is weird," or they just start giggling at the process. I even giggle at times watching this depending on the intensity level of the concern. I function as a support system and a guide in their communication.

One of the first things I voice with my couples is, "there must be a commitment to each other and the process that comes from being in counseling." In addition, to this, I provide an example of what this looks like. I liken it to the train system. There is one conductor in the front of the train and another in the middle. They (Conductor #1) are tasked with driving the train and I (Conductor #2) am responsible for making sure that the journey is smooth from one stop to another. As long as they commit to the process and continue driving the train, I will function gladly as the second conductor checking tickets, monitoring safety, and guiding. This illustration is something that gets their attention because in that moment they realize that I cannot do the work for them.

During the counseling series with a couple, I let them know that they will have to communicate with eye contact. It is something that I require and encourage. I explain that eye contact is a form of intimacy and that by having eye contact it also creates a sense of safety in your relationship and it fosters future discussions.

Communication with eye contact has the ability to create one of the most beautiful forms of foreplay. Looking in your partner's eyes when communicating allows them to see your soul, your heart, and your love for them in addition to hearing the words that are coming out of your mouth. It intensifies the genuineness that flows from you at any given moment. The more you communicate, the more comfortable you become looking at each other. Talking about sex can often get peoples' attention, so I am sure that by now knowing that it is a form of foreplay will be a good way to get you to do this more. At least, that is my intention.

Here are a few things you can do to ensure that eye contact is constant.

- 15 minutes before going to sleep, find space in your home where you both can just connect with one another. If your bedroom is the only place, that is fine. During that time, make sure you are facing one another.
- When you arrive home from work, take a moment to address each other with a kiss and some eye contact. Let your spouse know through your eye contact how you feel.
- When you are sexually intimate, try looking each other in the eyes the entire time or at least half of the time. Yes, I am telling you to leave the lights on.

We often find beauty in many things we see in life. Imagine the level of beauty you will be exposed to by taking the time to look into your spouses' eyes.

This is one intentional step that you should want to practice and incorporate into your marriage on a regular basis. It will enhance your relationship.

Exercise:

- At least once a week, schedule some time while in the bedroom where you both sit facing each other. While looking at each other, you may laugh a little until it becomes more comfortable. During this time, practice talking about your day, how you feel about one another, things you would like to do, etc. It can be a variety of topics, but make sure there is some time to focus on your relationship, feelings, and love for one another.
- Closeout this time together with prayer and a moment of thankfulness to solidify your bond.

Notes:

_____

_____

_____

_____

Way #6:

Touch, Touch, & Touch Some More

Touch, Touch, & Touch Some More

> ***Romans 15:5-6 (NIV):*** *"May the God who gives endurance and encouragement give you the same attitude of mind toward each other that Christ Jesus had, so that with one mind and one voice you may glorify the God and Father of our Lord Jesus Christ."*

Touch, Touch, Touch, Touch, Touch, Touch!!! I am repeating it because I am trying to get your attention again. Within every relationship, touch should be a standard of affection.

There is something so powerful about touching. My husband and I touch often, whether it is holding hands, holding each other at night, grabbing a hug and a kiss when we walk past each other, and/or letting our feet touch when we are in bed.

I don't know about you, but my husband's touch symbolizes our connectedness. Even in moments when we may not be fully in sync, touch is something that is constant. He expresses that it is the same for him. He loves when I hold his face in the palm of my hands when I kiss him or tell him how much I love him.

Here is some more mushy stuff. When we both have to travel alone, we find it extremely hard to rest at night because we are so used to being near and touching one another. You would think that we were born married to each other and had never been apart. However, that is not the case. What this has shown me is that touch for both of us means a great deal. Our love for one another has strengthened over the years and touch is a way that keeps us connected even when there are no words shared. As a result of touch, we feel loved, wanted, protected, connected, and sexy. Yes, sexy. There is nothing greater than knowing that your spouse loves touching and holding you.

Every one of us would like to feel loved, wanted, protected, connected, and sexy. I liked those words so much, I chose to write them again. (This is your cue to chuckle as I am already laughing). Being touched is something that should be implemented often.

Touching is not isolated to sexual intercourse and the confines of your bedroom. We are talking about being fulfilled sexually in your relationship and understanding that you and your mate can define what that looks like.

Intimacy is reserved for your marriage and the two of you alone. It is important and should be talked about. It is also something that you should be excited about.

Being touched or getting ready for intimacy means that preparation may be necessary and intentional. I am referring to the smell goods, sexy lingerie, candles, and setting the mood. Know that this is good. Recognize your time of intimacy as precious and wonderful.

There is power in touch. This is something that can be easily implemented. As I stated earlier, it is not isolated to the bedroom. You can start with holding hands when you are out and about shopping, in the movies, or even at home watching television. Try kissing every time you walk by one another. My husband and I do something called the 10-second kiss. We do it in passing or sometimes, I will go to the family room, climb in the lounge chair on top of him, hold his face and kiss him for 10 seconds. At the end of the kiss, we both say, "10!" It works for us. Find things that work for you.

This is your opportunity to increase your affection and intimacy. Be as creative as you would like and remember that touching is not isolated to the bedroom. All of this connectivity through touch can lead to a stronger intimate relationship. Try it. You will not be disappointed. It is simple and powerful.

Exercise:

- Holding hands is something we generally think of when we think of touch, but I want you to think outside of the box. Ladies, when your husband is driving, reach over and rub the back of his neck. Men, while driving, reach over and touch your wife's leg.

- While entering or exiting an event, place your arms around each other's waist. Make sure you lean into each other a little while doing so. It implies your approval of the moment.

Notes:

Way #7:

Create Comfort in Conflict

Create Comfort in Conflict

Colossians 4:6 (NIV): Let your conversation be always full of grace, seasoned with salt, so that you may know how to answer everyone."

In speaking of communication, most people believe that they are great communicators simply because they perceive themselves as having the ability to say what they feel at any point in time. What they have failed to realize is that even though they expressed themselves freely, the other party is unable to receive it because of how the message has been delivered. This is something that can create conflict and misunderstanding in a marriage.

Conflict is often perceived from a negative viewpoint. I see it as an opportunity to communicate effectively in resolving a concern whether held by one or both parties. Conflict is not something I love, but it is something that I embrace.

In my work with couples, I've noticed that they all have this perception that conflict is bad and something to be avoided like it is an actual plague from some foreign planet. From the time I start my work with couples, I highlight that communicating freely does not mean that you are communicating effectively. Sometimes you are just being vocal. This is either met with an acknowledgement or puzzled looks. In that moment, I explain how communicating effectively can change things for the betterment of the relationship.

As a couples' therapist, I utilize the Prepare/Enrich® assessment tool and curriculum which can be used for seriously dating, engaged and married couples. Prepare/Enrich® has a history of 35 plus years of providing assessments to over 4 million couples. It is considered an evidenced-based model that I trust in working with couples. The assessment results show the areas of strengths and areas needing growth. The results are solely based on how the couples respond to the statements on the assessment. When sharing the assessment results with the couples, they are asked if they agree or disagree with the results. They often agree with the results and express some relief in being validated and affirmed about their perceptions of their relationship.

I have noticed that it is not uncommon for many couples to rate low in the areas of communication and conflict resolution. These areas can potentially impact the ratings of other areas in the assessment.

This information also helps to guide the couple's sessions. No matter which assessment area is focused on each week, it always links back to the couples' ability to communicate and resolve conflict effectively.

The couples are then taught the importance of communication and how to respond to conflict appropriately.

Conflict is not only an opportunity to communicate, but it is also about helping the person initiating the communication to feel safe in sharing their concern(s). There is much to be said about feeling safe in a relationship. Every person wants to be heard, understood, and validated.

In conflict resolution, it is important that both parties know that it is safe to express concerns without feeling misunderstood or judged.

I often encourage my couples to work on their delivery of the message when communicating a concern by using "I" statements. It is imperative that communication is done in a way where the other person can receive and understand fully. On the end of the person receiving the message, you must be willing to listen from the beginning to the end of the concern being communicated. Try not to rev those engines with a quick response or comeback. It is not about you proving you are right and that they are wrong.

Yes, I am pointing out those individuals who will give the appearance that they are listening, but in actuality, they have been practicing in their mind what they are going to say, as soon as their mate is finished speaking. If that is you, let's make a vow today to not do that. Just focus on listening to their heart and the message. Be ready to acknowledge and let them know you hear them by repeating what has been communicated. Keep in mind that you do not always have to be right when working through a conflict. The goal is to understand each other and work together through the conflict.

Allowing a person to communicate their concerns, can provide great satisfaction in a relationship. It also creates an opportunity to foster ongoing communication about anything and everything if you allow it to be.

So, if you are attempting to create comfort in conflict, remember the importance of listening (carefully and without judgment), showing understanding, and validating.

Communicating effectively and in a safe place, will strengthen your relationship, as well as your comfort level in sharing through conflict.

I chose to write this section last because it is the most challenging and critical for couples and yet the most important.

The 7 Simple Ways to Shape your Marriage are all interconnected. One strengthens the other and no one is more important than another. These are only seven of many, many ways that you can use to shape your relationship.

It is my belief that you can accomplish these areas when intentionally committing to do things differently and purposefully. Now, that you have received this information, please, Go Forth and Conquer! Own It Like A Boss! Be intentional about the one you love and the way you love. In doing so, you will get what you need especially the love and connection you seek!! Selah.

Exercise:

- Schedule a time each week to have a weekly meeting to discuss things of importance in your marriage and home. By having ongoing communication, it increases your level of comfort in communicating.

Notes:

_____

_____

_____

_____

_____

_____

_____

_____

_____

Epilogue

My heart's desire in writing this book was to strengthen couples by imploring very simple yet powerful strategies that have been helpful to my marriage. Initially, I would pray and ask God to just change my husband and he would do the same. In order for prayer to work, I had to put my faith to work by working on myself first and walking with my husband through this process. A partnership of faith had and always has to exist. What seemed to be difficult, became a blessing. We both became even more intentional in how we maneuver in our marriage. Every day is filled with another opportunity or challenge that we must endure. We are not exempt from challenges and trials that test us. However, because of our love, we are intentionally and purposefully walking through our journey together.

In being married, and working with the amazing couples that have trusted me on their journey, I have so much joy in knowing that couples can be strengthened when there is a commitment present. I believe in and honor marriage. It is my ongoing mission to help strengthen marriages. It is also my prayer that I continue this work. Selah.

References

Building Blocks to A Strong Marriage
Copyright © 1986, 2001, RBC Ministries,
Grand Rapids, Michigan, pp 19, 25, 26

Intentional. (2018). In Merriam-webster.com.
Retrieved from https://www.merriam-
webster.com/dictionary/intentional

The Power of a Praying® Wife, Stormie
Omartian Copyright © 1997, 2004 Harvest
House Publishers, Eugene Oregon

Prepare/Enrich®, www.prepare-enrich.com

Unless otherwise indicated, all Scripture
quotations are taken from the New
International Version (NIV)

About the Author

Sharon J. Lawrence
LCSW-C, LCSW, ACSW, EAS-C, CAMS-II, BC-TMH

Mrs. Lawrence is a Licensed Clinical Social Worker (LCSW-C/ LCSW) (MD/VA), Certified Anger Management Specialists-II (CAMS-II), Certified Prepare/Enrich® Facilitator/Trainer, Certified Life Coach, Board Certified-TeleMental Health Provider (BC-TMH), an Approved Clinical Supervisor in Social Work (MD) and credentialed as an Employee Assistance Specialist-Clinician. She also holds a Certificate in Christian Ministries from the Evangel Bible College in Upper Marlboro, MD. She has over 15 years of experience working with children, adults, couples and families within the following settings: mental health, substance abuse, foster care, family court, and developmental disabilities.

Mrs. Lawrence is the owner of Selah Wellness & Therapeutic Services, LLC, where she practices as a Therapist for Therapists, Professionals and Couples. Her passion is to improve the lives of clinicians and professionals who manage the day to day responsibility of caring for others. It has been proven that this type of care can produce secondary trauma in addition to discovering and revealing past trauma and mental health challenges.

Mrs. Lawrence is committed to helping couples strengthen and revive their relationships through counseling using the Prepare/Enrich® assessment and curriculum. She provides both short and long-term counseling using Cognitive Behavioral Therapy, Solution Focused Therapy, Motivational Interviewing, and Eye Movement Desensitization Reprocessing (EMDR).

Mrs. Lawrence is also a Speaker, Presenter, Trainer and Blogger for subject matter topics related to mental health education, marital enrichment, self-care and motivating entrepreneurs. She has a YouTube Channel called My Selah Wellness focused on motivating individuals towards emotional wellness. She is the creator of Desserts & Discussions: The Tour 2018 which focuses on speaking to area churches, businesses and organizations on topics related to mental health, women's empowerment, and personal growth.

28677172R00046

Made in the USA
Columbia, SC
15 October 2018